I0163246

# Do You Sit on the Potty?

Written and illustrated by

Candice Hyman

Copyright © 2015 Candice Hyman-thekhaidencehouse.com

All rights reserved. No part of this publication may be reproduced, distributed, or transmitted in any form or by any means, including photocopying, recording, or other electronic or mechanical methods, without the prior written permission of the publisher, except in the case of brief quotations embodied in critical reviews and certain other noncommercial uses permitted by copyright law.

Published by The Khaidence House Publishing Co.

info@thekhaidencehouse.com

ISBN-13: 978-0692470695
ISBN-10: 0692470697

## DEDICATION

This dedication belongs to my boys, J and K. Remember that it takes hard work to get what you want out of life. Just figure out what you want and the steps you need to take to get there. Always remember the "why", because it will remind you of the reasons of why your so passionate to get to that thing that you want so very badly.

With Love,
Mommy

**COMING SOON**

A Toddlers Prayer

Brush, Brush My Teeth

Everybody Bath Time

Light Switch Chronicles

## ACKNOWLEDGMENTS

Thank you to my friends and family! You folks give the best advice and I love you for that!

Hi boys and girls! Are you ready to take the Potty Test?

Does a **F**ireman sit on the potty?

Yes...
You're right! A Fireman does sit on the potty.

Does a **T**eacher sit on the potty?

Yes...
Excellent! A Teacher does sit on the potty.

Does a puppy pee-pee in the potty?

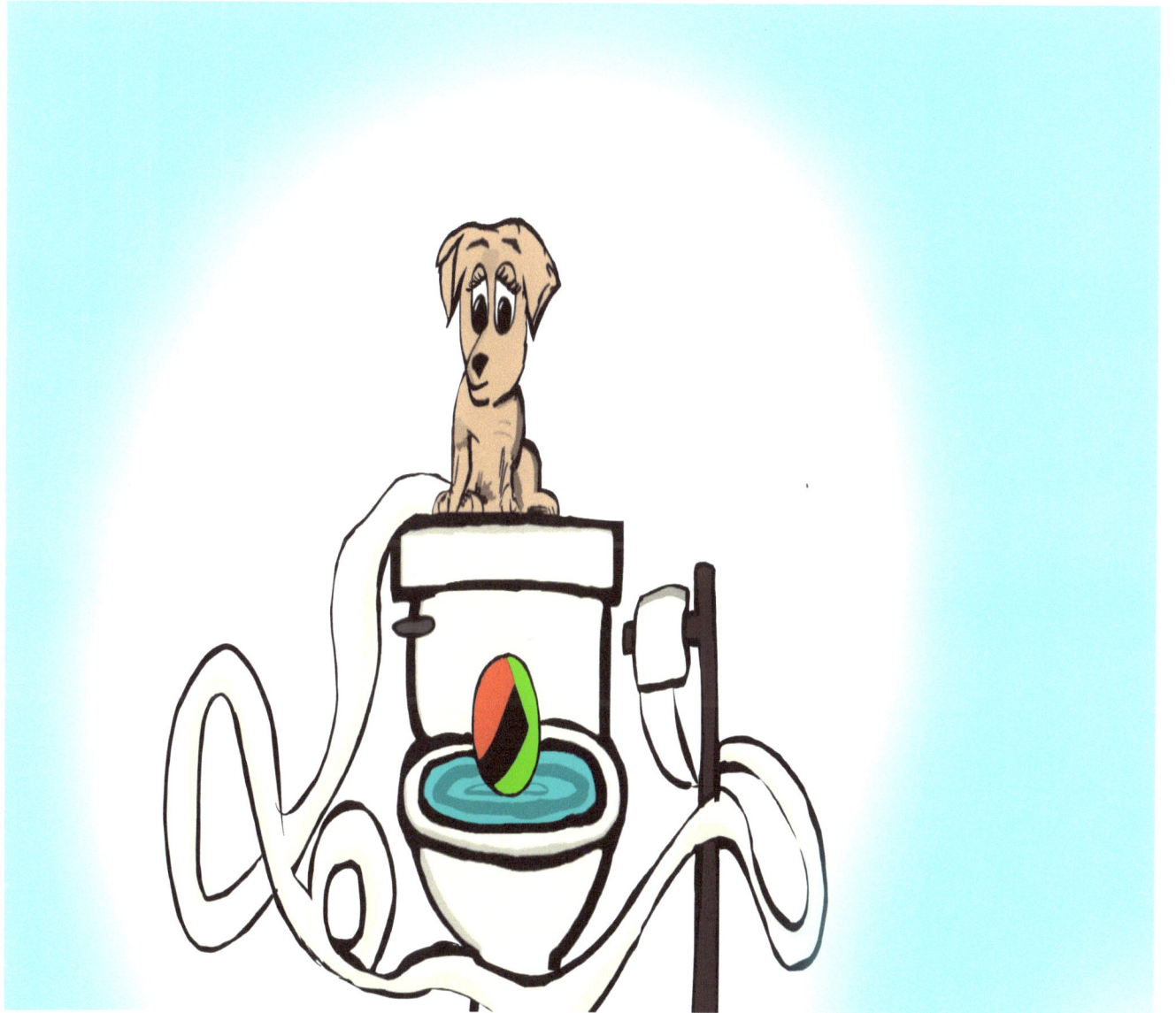

No...
Good job! A puppy does not pee-pee in the potty.

Does a **B**asketball player sit on the potty?

Yes...
That's right! A Basketball player does sit on the potty.

Does Mommy sit on the potty?

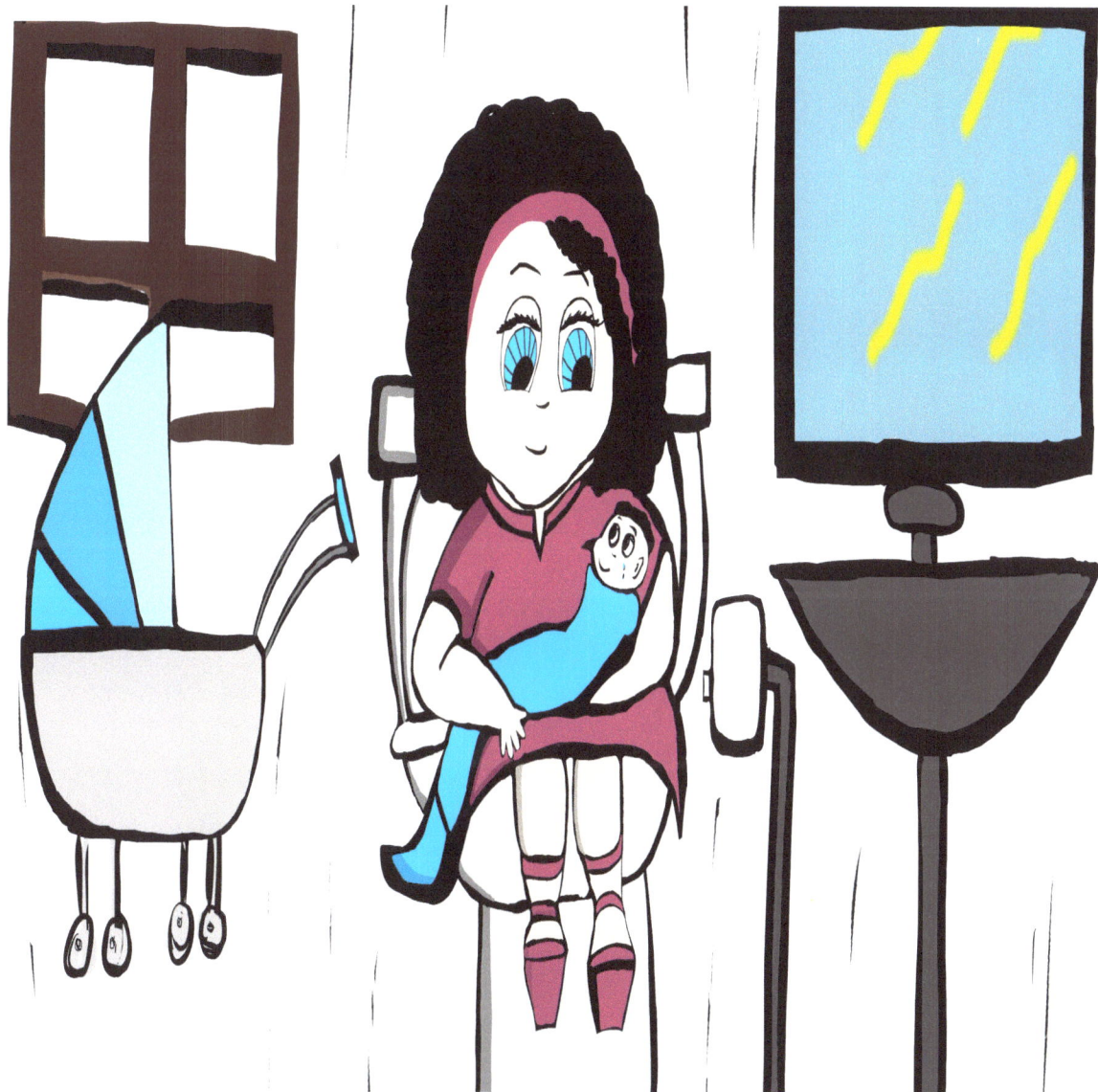

Yes...
Perfect! Mommy does sit on the potty!

Using the potty is just part of growing up.

It also makes mommy and daddy very happy!

If a Fireman, Teacher, Basketball player and a Mommy can sit on the potty, you can too!

Can I ask you a question?

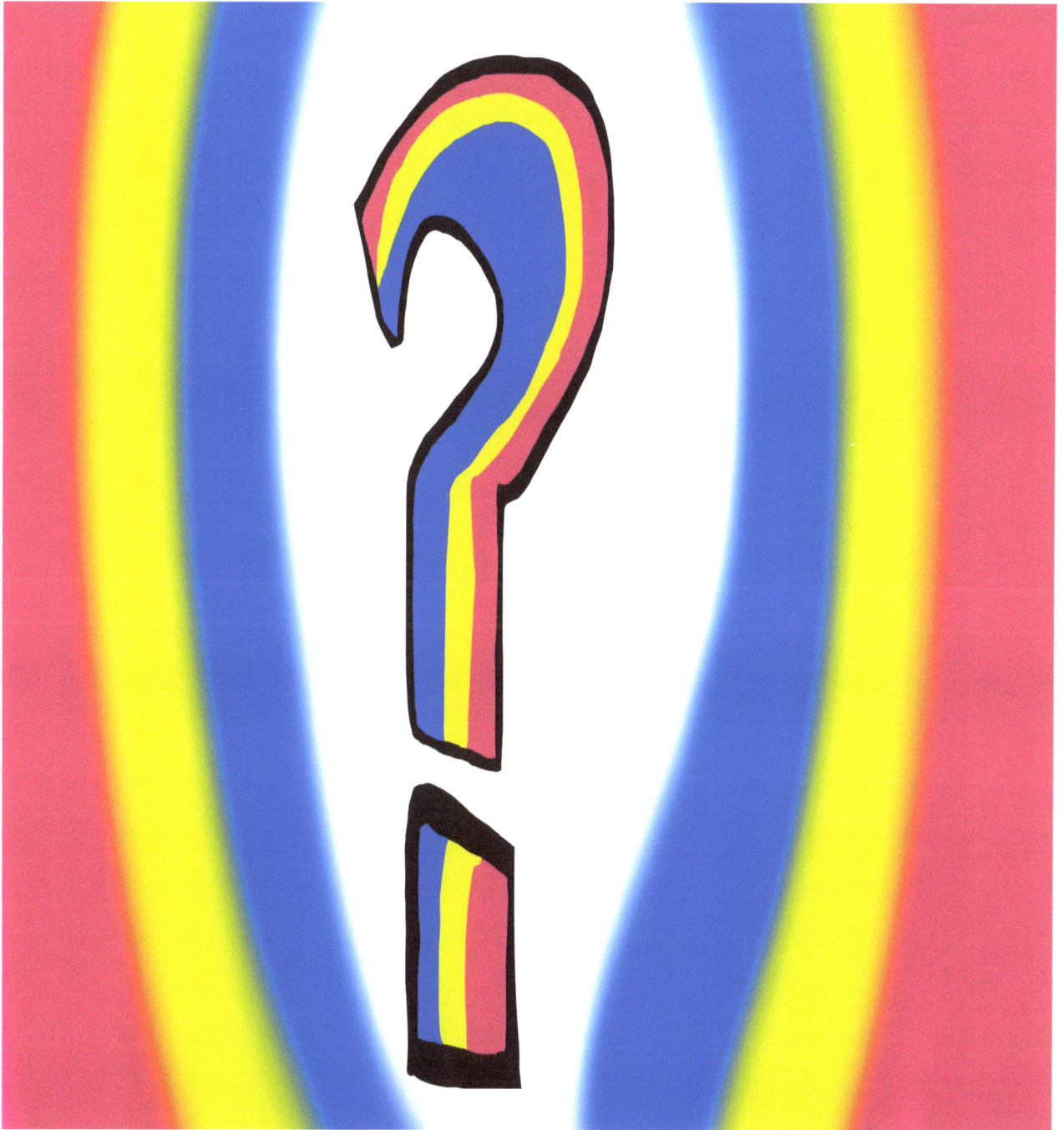

Do you sit on the potty?

YOU!

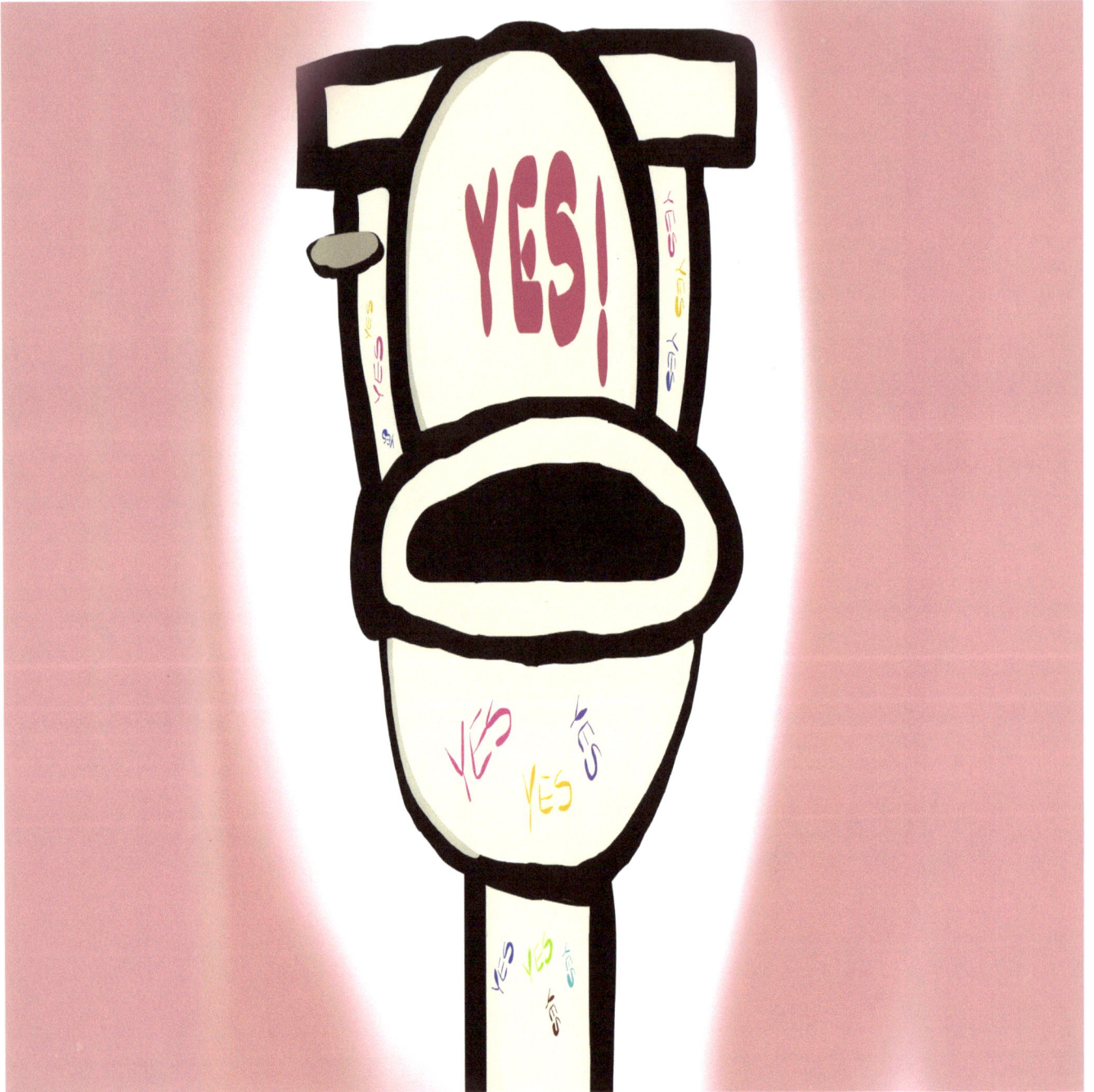

Congratulations boys and girls! You have passed the Potty Test!

The End

www.ingramcontent.com/pod-product-compliance
Lightning Source LLC
Chambersburg PA
CBHW042104040426
42448CB00002B/136